T0405886

NOTORIOUS PIRATES GRAPHICS

# CHING SHIH
## FAMOUS PIRATE COMMANDER

by Stephanie Peters ✦ illustrated by Lia Liao

CAPSTONE PRESS
a capstone imprint

Published by Capstone Press, an imprint of Capstone
1710 Roe Crest Drive, North Mankato, Minnesota 56003
capstonepub.com



Library of Congress Cataloging-in-Publication Data
Names: Peters, Stephanie, author. | Liao, Lia, illustrator.
Title: Ching Shih, famous pirate commander / by Stephanie Peters ; illustrated by Lia Liao.
Description: North Mankato, Minnesota : Capstone Press, [2025] |
Series: Notorious pirates graphics | Includes bibliographical references. |
Audience: Ages 9–11 | Audience: Grades 4–6 | Summary: "Born poor in rural China, Ching Shih's early life was full of challenges. But she would grow to become one of the most powerful pirates the world had ever seen. She made a name for herself using her intelligence and cunning. Learn how Ching Shih became a famous pirate commander—and the terror of the South China Sea—in a graphic novel filled with adventure and intrigue."—Provided by publisher.
Identifiers: LCCN 2023046198 (print) | LCCN 2023046199 (ebook) |
ISBN 9781669069577 (hardcover) | ISBN 9781669069522 (paperback) |
ISBN 9781669069539 (pdf) | ISBN 9781669069546 (epub) |
ISBN 9781669069553 (kindle edition)
Subjects: LCSH: Zheng, Shi, 1775–1844—Juvenile literature. | Zheng, Shi, 1775–1844—Comic books, strips, etc. | Women pirates—China—Biography—Juvenile literature. | Women pirates—China—Biography—Comic books, strips, etc. | LCGFT: Biographical comics. | Graphic novels.
Classification: LCC DS756.23.Z47 P48 2025 (print) | LCC DS756.23.Z47 (ebook) | DDC 951/.033092 [B]—dc23/eng/20240205
LC record available at https://lccn.loc.gov/2023046198
LC ebook record available at https://lccn.loc.gov/2023046199

Editorial Credits
Editor: Alison Deering; Designer: Elijah Blue; Production Specialist: Tori Abraham



Printed and bound in the USA. 5853

# CONTENTS

# INTRODUCTION

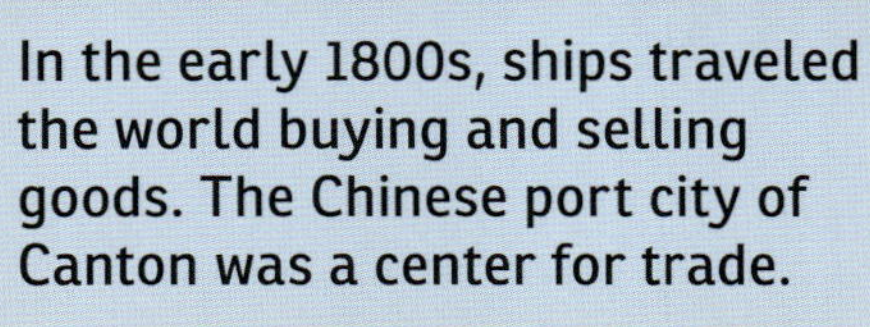


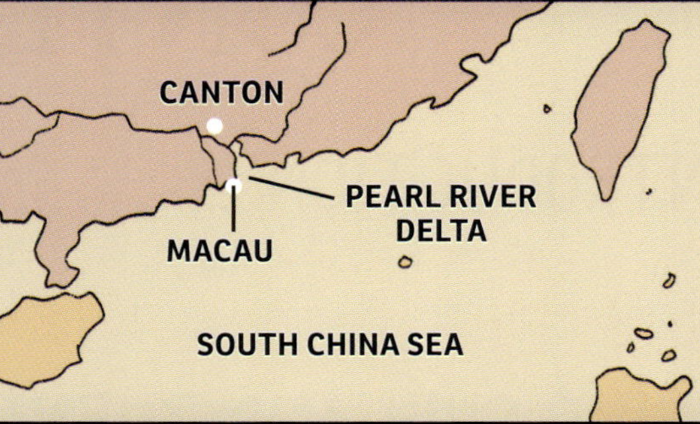

She almost always got what she wanted.
At the height of her power, Ching Shih was known as the Terror of South China.
More treasure awaits. Sail on!

CHAPTER 1

# CHING SHIH AND ZHENG YI

I know of a ship you can plunder. But my information isn't free.
She's beautiful and smart!
Zheng Yi asked Ching Shih to marry him.
Only if I can be your equal. I want half of all we plunder.
Agreed!
Let's find a ship to raid!

Zheng Yi and his pirate fleet had long been feared by traders from every nation.
Ching Shih became just as feared.
FIRE!
BOOM!
She liked getting rich.
Your tea will bring in lots of money. For me.
She liked being in charge too.
Lock him up.

Sometimes, she made money by kidnapping rich people.

Who will pay the ransom to free him?

We will!

Ching Shih and Zheng Yi's fleet grew. Soon, they had 200 ships.

We can't outrun them!

We're trapped!

Many crews joined after being raided.
Welcome aboard.

The only real danger was from rival pirates.
Ching Shih's loot will be mine!

Rival pirates rarely made it onto Ching Shih's ships.
You dare try to steal from me?
But if they did . . .
CLANG!
BANG!
AIYEE!
They lost in the end.
I'll let you go. But don't cross me again.

After a time, the rivalries ended. An alliance was born.
Rebels in Vietnam were fighting for a new government. They paid Chinese pirates to fight with them.
We need more weapons!
One of you will find guns. The other will get them to my ship.
And then you bring them to the rebels.
The pirates fought for the rebels for months.
But the rebels were defeated.

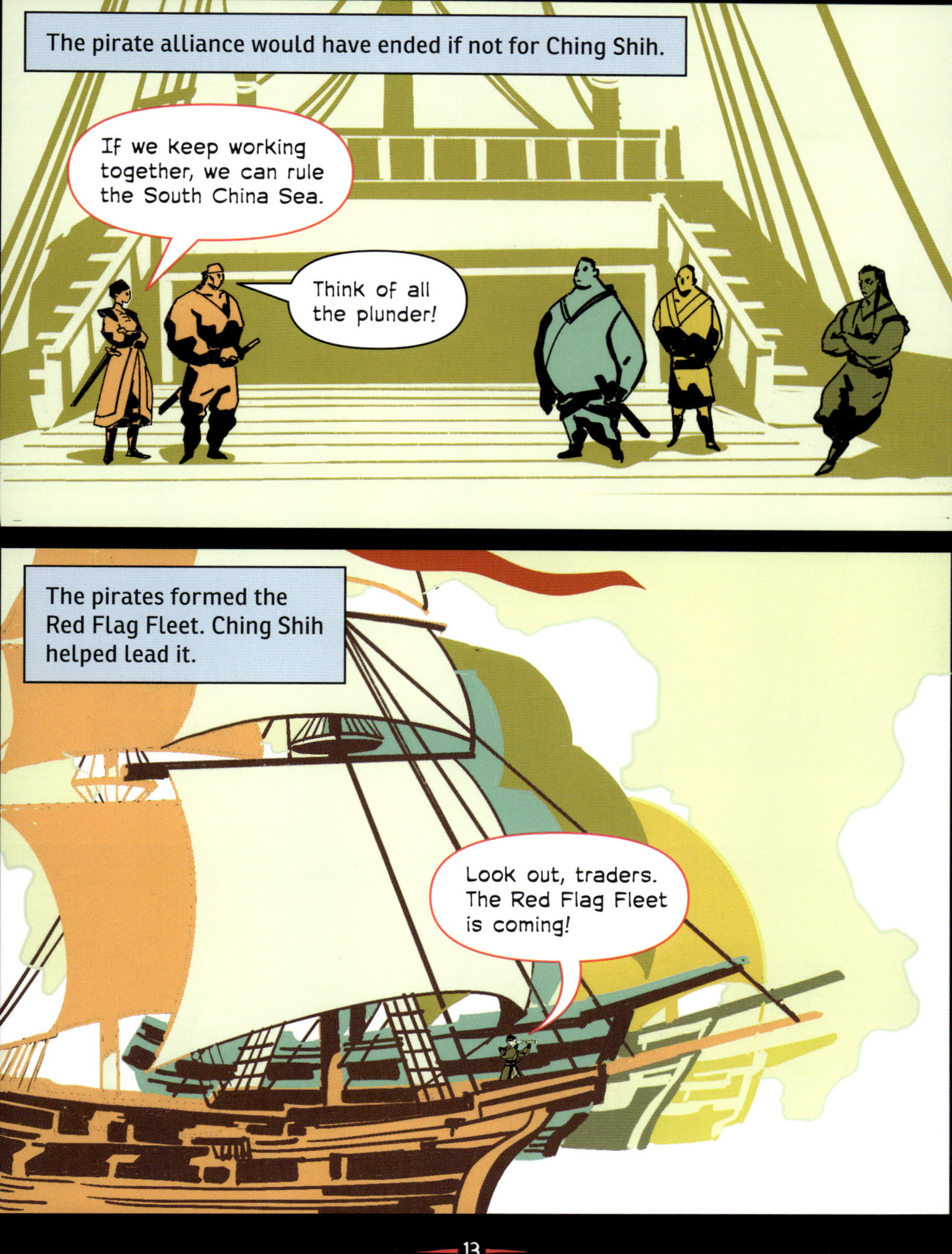
The pirate alliance would have ended if not for Ching Shih.
If we keep working together, we can rule the South China Sea.
Think of all the plunder!
The pirates formed the Red Flag Fleet. Ching Shih helped lead it.
Look out, traders. The Red Flag Fleet is coming!

## CHAPTER 2

# THE RED FLAG FLEET

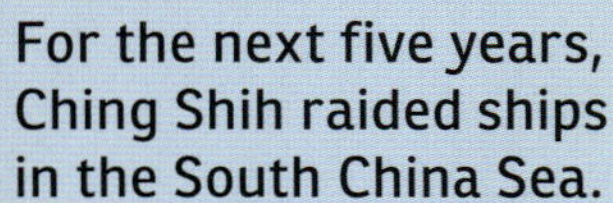

There is no escape from the Red Flag Fleet!

Sometimes, she destroyed ships after robbing them.

Zheng Yi's sudden death put the future of the Red Flag Fleet at risk.

Perhaps we should go our own ways.

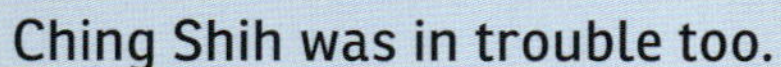

Ching Shih made sure her crew stayed loyal.

Loot will be split equally among us all!

HOORAY!

HOORAY!

Under her command, the Red Flag Fleet grew stronger than ever before.

What next?

You'll see.

Ching Shih focused on building the fleet's wealth and power.

Chase the cargo ships till they run into rocks!

Her plans usually worked.

SCR-A-A-APE!

We've got you now.

Those who didn't take Ching Shih's deal still paid a price.

But Ching Shih was fair. If she failed to protect those who paid, she gave their money back.

Your loss is my loss.

In 1808, Ching Shih came up with a bold plan.
We'll steal from the emperor's military.

The army was busy fighting. The navy was weak. This made bases on the coast easy targets.
We'll dress as soldiers to get inside.

Hurry into the base, soldier!

Attack!
AHH!

Take their guns!

Ching Shih also stole
from navy warships.

In all, she stole 200
cannons and 300 guns.

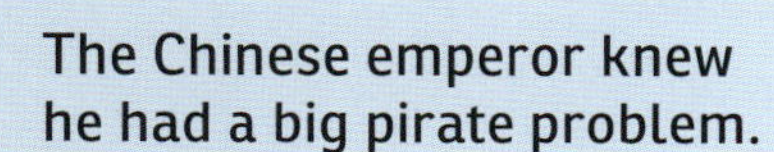
The Chinese emperor knew
he had a big pirate problem.

Another raid?

Ching Shih and the
Red Flag Fleet
must be stopped!

## CHAPTER 3

# THE TERROR VS. THE EMPEROR

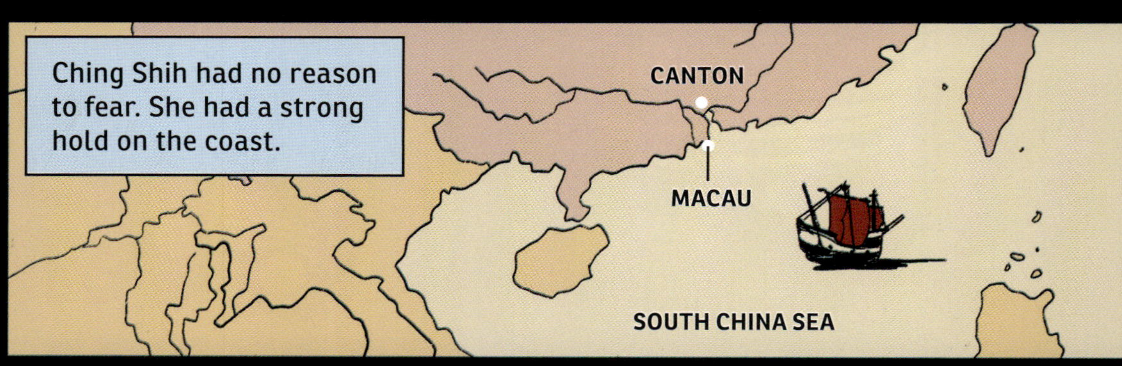

Losing a warship was bad for the navy.
Easy.
Losing trade was bad for the emperor.
Trade brings in money. And I need money to stay in power!
I must *destroy* the Red Flag Fleet!

Thanks to her spies, Ching Shih learned of the emperor's plans.
PSST-PSST!
He's sending 35 warships? We'll be ready.
Those ships have red flags! After them!
Faster!
Steady, men.
You're trapped now, pirate!
But the pirates weren't trapped. The navy was!
Take them down.

The battle lasted for 16 hours.
BOOM!
BOOM!
BOOM!
When it was over, all the emperor's warships were at the bottom of the sea.
Face it. The navy will never stop us!

Ching Shih kept testing the navy.
Those aren't Red Flag Fleet pirates. But they will be if we help them.
Sail your ships to their right. Then you, take yours to their left.
Yes, Captain!
What are you going to do?
You'll see.

The warships could only go one way to escape.
Ching Shih was waiting for them!
FIRE!
BANG!
BANG!
KA-POW!
Thank you, Captain!
Thank me by joining my fleet.
We will!

The emperor attacked again. He sent 100 warships.
Don't bother returning if you fail.
GULP!

But Ching Shih outsmarted the navy at every turn.
Go behind them, then fire!

If we can't sail close enough to fight, we'll swim instead.

Use your swords, knives, fists, legs . . .

Just take them down!
SLICE!
OOF!
CLANG!

I told you. You can't stop me!
Ching Shih's fleet sank more than 60 warships in that battle.
The emperor might rule China. But I rule the South China Sea!
But she lost ships too. And soon, others would come after the Red Flag Fleet.

CHAPTER 4

# THE BATTLE OF TIGER'S MOUTH

After six weeks, the Red Flag Fleet set sail. They soon found a Portuguese trade ship.
Take the cargo.
What about the ship and its crew?
Both are weak. Destroy them.

Word of Ching Shih's actions reached Portugal's ruler.
Send six warships to protect Macau and end that pirate!
Ching Shih learned of the attack.
Ready our best ships. We sail at dawn.
Prepare for battle, men!

The Red Flag Fleet fought hard.

Fire everything we have!

WHUMP!

BOOM! BOOM!

Ching Shih was not used to losing.
We have more ships now!
The Portuguese have more too—60 Chinese warships.
Once again, the pirates attacked with everything they had.
BOOM!
BOOM!
POW!

But once again, the Portuguese won.
What did we lose?
Fifteen ships. Too many men to count.
The Red Flag Fleet is still strong. We *will* defeat our enemies!

Ching Shih led ships into the Pearl River Delta.
They're retreating to the Tiger's Mouth.
Follow. We'll trap them there.
Trapping the enemy in shallow water had worked before.
But this time, Ching Shih was outsmarted.

Ching Shih's plan didn't work.

For the first time ever, the Red Flag Fleet was in big trouble.

# CHAPTER 5
# THE END OF THE RED FLAG FLEET

Put away your weapons.
I want to talk.
Well, pirate.
Are you here
to surrender?
No. I am here
to bargain.

The emperor's men were used to getting their way.
You will surrender.
We will take your ships.
Your pirates will live on land. Anyone caught raiding ships will be put to death.
But they had never dealt with Ching Shih.
I will keep 80 ships and 5,000 men.
What?!
In April 1810, the talks ended.
The two sides finally signed a peace treaty.
Gather the crew.

The Red Flag Fleet is no more. But you can join the military.
What?
Or you can start a new life on land. You get to keep all your loot—and your lives!
HOORAY!
HOORAY!
And so, the Red Flag Fleet's violent rule came to a peaceful end.

The treaty called for Ching Shih to give up her fleet.
I will miss the life of a pirate.
But she kept her plunder. She used her riches to move to Canton.
Welcome to the best gambling house in the city! Good luck!
You'll need it.
Instead of stealing, she cheated men out of their money.

Ching Shih lived the rest of her days in Canton. She never set sail again.
But no other pirate—male or female—was ever as successful or as feared as Ching Shih, the Terror of South China.

# MORE ABOUT CHING SHIH

- *Ching Shih* means "the widow of Ching." She's also known as Shih Yang, Shi Xainggu, Cheng I Sao, and Zheng Yi Sao.

- Ching Shih was born in a village outside of Canton. Nothing is known about her family or life as a child.

- Ching Shih had more than 1,800 ships and 70,000 men under her command. The famous pirate Blackbeard, who was active around the same time, had just 4 ships and 300 men.

- Ching Shih had three sons. Two were with Zheng Yi and one with Zhang Bao.

- Ching Shih once destroyed several of the emperor's warships as they were being built.

- Ching Shih has been a character in popular movies and fiction. She is shown as a powerful pirate who inspires respect and fear.

- Much of what we know about Ching Shih and the Red Flag Fleet comes from an Englishman she captured. She held him for nine months before letting him go.

# GLOSSARY

**alliance** (uh-LY-uhns)—an agreement between groups to work together

**armada** (ar-MAH-duh)—a large fleet of warships

**emperor** (EM-per-er)—the male ruler of an empire or group of countries

**fleet** (FLEET)—a group of ships under one command

**heir** (AIR)—someone who has been or will be left a title, property, or money

**plunder** (PLUHN-der)—to steal things by force, often during battle; also, valuable items stolen during battle

**ransom** (RAN-suhm)—money or objects that are demanded before someone who is being held captive can be set free

**retreat** (rih-TREET)—to move out of battle or away from an enemy

**rival** (RY-vuhl)—someone whom a person competes against

**storehouse** (STOHR-hous)—a building for storing goods

**surrender** (suh-REN-der)—to give up and stop fighting

**treaty** (TREE-tee)—an official agreement between two or more groups or countries

# OTHER BOOKS IN THIS SERIES

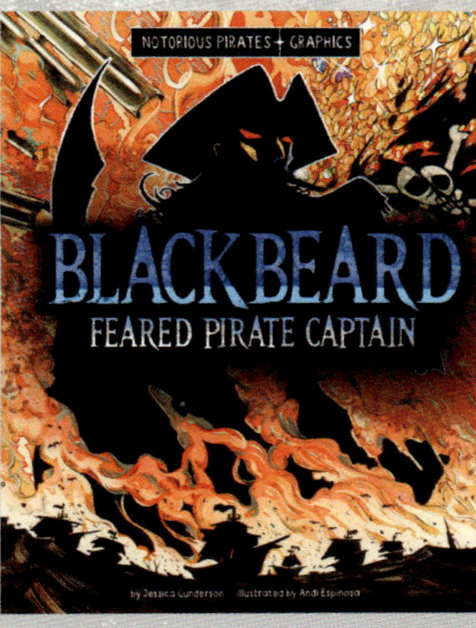


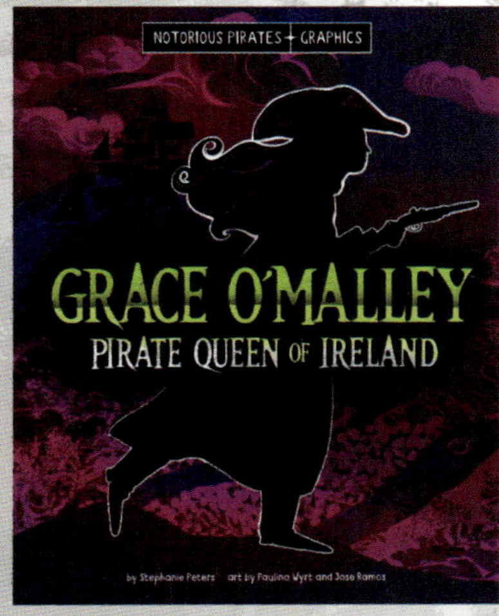


# INTERNET SITES

*Academic Kids: Ching Shih*
academickids.com/encyclopedia/index.php/Ching_Shih

*KidPid: Who Was Ching Shih?*
kidpid.com/who-was-ching-shih/

*National Geographic: Episode 11: Queens of the High Seas*
nationalgeographic.com/podcasts/overheard/article
/queens-of-the-high-seas

# ABOUT THE CREATORS

**STEPHANIE PETERS** is a freelance children's book writer with a diverse portfolio of published titles featuring princesses and swamp monsters, inspirational men and heroic dogs, sports of all sorts, and Greek mythology. An avid reader, workout enthusiast, and animal lover, Stephanie is a firm believer that our words and actions matter. She lives in Mansfield, Massachusetts, with her husband, Dan; an aging cat; and two rabbits.

**LIA LIAO** is an illustrator who currently resides in New York. She was educated as a psychologist until 2020 when she decided to pursue a career in illustration. She feels the meaning in different languages is often lost in translation. Therefore, Lia chooses to express her feelings and emotions through art. She combines her knowledge in psychology with her skills in illustration to create her own unique style, which is rational and logical while at the same time emotionally striking.